Rainbows

Written by
Jill McDougall

Contents

Rainbows	2
Rainbow Colours	4
What are Rainbows?	6
Sun and Water	8
Rainbow Facts	10
Spotting Rainbows	12
Rainbow Print	14
Colour Chart	16

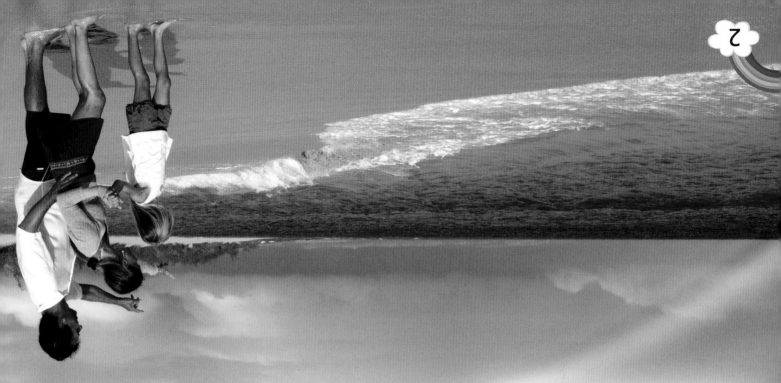

Rainbows

Rainbows can happen when there is sun and rain.

You can see lots of colours.

Rainbow Colours

A rainbow has seven colours.

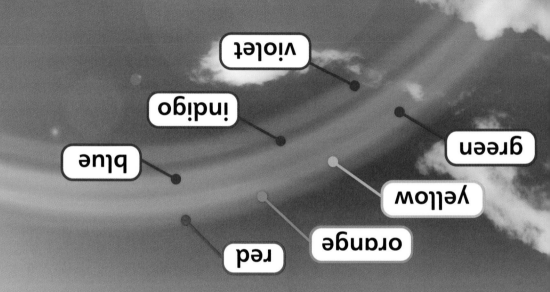

violet

indigo

green

blue

yellow

orange

red

Rainbow colours are fun!

What are Rainbows?

1. It rains.
2. The sun comes out.
3. The sunlight hits drops of rain.
4. You see a rainbow.

rain drops

sun

6

You might see a rainbow after a storm.

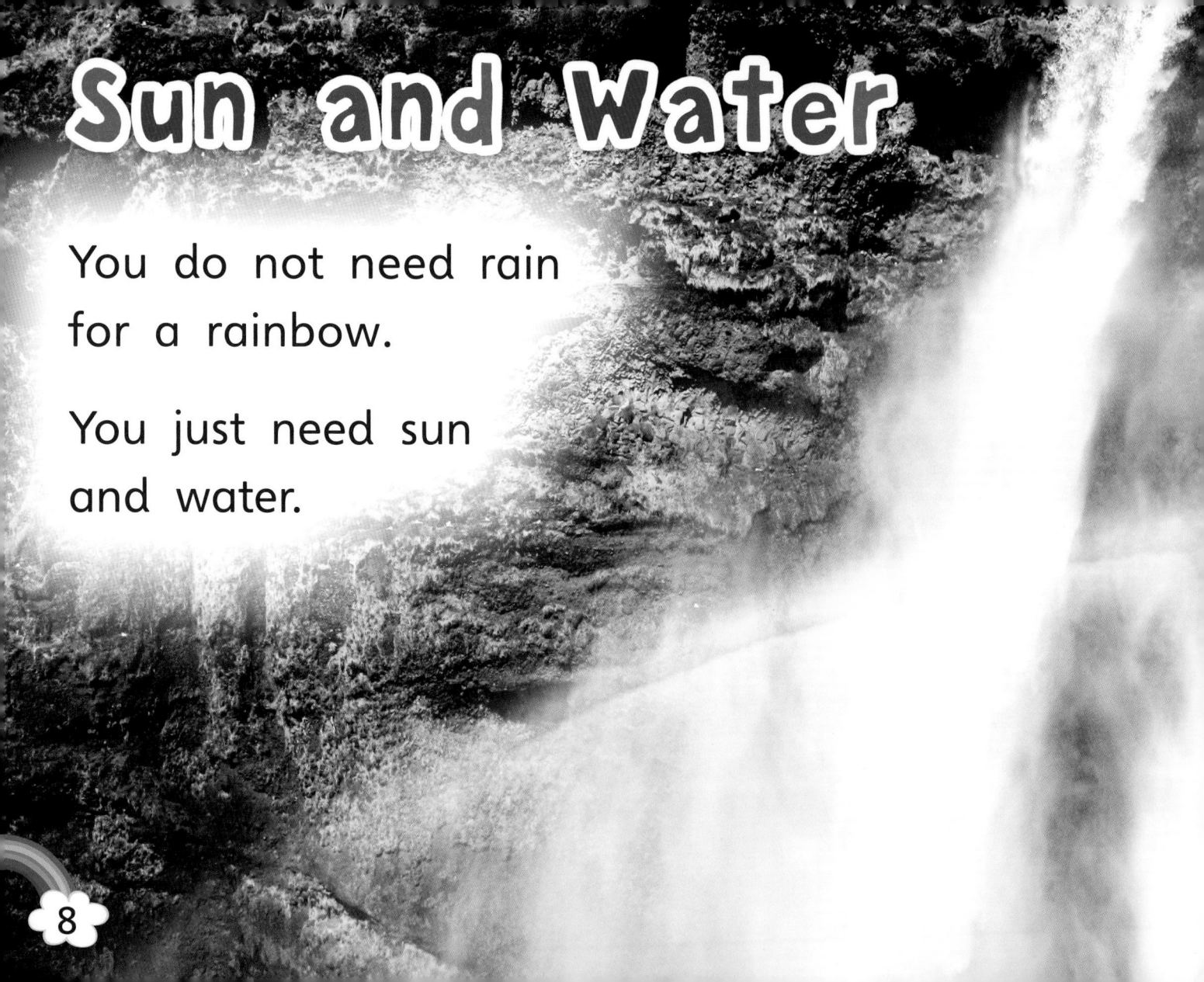

Sun and Water

You do not need rain for a rainbow.

You just need sun and water.

8

You might see a rainbow in the garden.

Rainbow Facts

You cannot go under a rainbow.

You cannot get to the end of a rainbow.

Spotting Rainbows

Look at this.

There is not just one rainbow.

You can see rainbows at night, too.
They look like this.

Rainbow Print

1

Get some paint in rainbow colours.

2

Dip a hand in the paint.

3

Press your
hand down.

It is a rainbow!

Colour chart

red

orange

yellow

green

blue

indigo

violet